Jim's house in 1874

Written by Gill Munton

Speed Sounds

Consonants   *Ask children to say the sounds.*

f	l	m	n	r	s	v	z	sh	th	ng
ff	ll	mm	nn	rr	ss	ve	zz			nk
	(le)		kn		(se)		se			
					ce		s			

b	c	d	g	h	j	p	(qu)	t	w	x	y	(ch)
bb	k	dd	gg		g	pp		tt	wh			(tch)
	ck				ge							

Each box contains one sound but sometimes more than one grapheme.
*Focus graphemes for this story are **circled**.*

Vowels

Ask children to say the sounds in and out of order.

a	e ea	i	o	u	ay	ee y	igh	ow
at	hen	in	on	up	day	see	high	blow

oo	oo	ar	or oor ore	air	ir	ou	oy
zoo	look	car	for	fair	whirl	shout	boy

5

Story Green Words

Ask children to read the words first in Fred Talk and then say the word.

Sid   Patch   room   found   mouse   horse
lamp   bowl   jug   lav   top   couch   proud

Ask children to say the syllables and then read the whole word.

kitch|en   man|gle*   scrap|book   gar|den
scull|er|y*   bed|room   bath|room

Ask children to read the root first and then the whole word with the suffix.

dress → dresses   squeeze → squeezes
song → songs   rock → rocking
spin → spinning

*Challenge Words

Vocabulary Check

Discuss the meaning (as used in the non-fiction text) after the children have read the word.

	definition
scullery	a room for washing clothes and dishes
scrapbook	a book for keeping small pieces of paper, such as pictures cut from magazines
oil lamp	a light that uses burning oil, not electricity
lav	short for lavatory, which means 'toilet'
couch	a long, soft seat or sofa

Red Words

Ask children to practise reading the words across the rows, down the columns and in and out of order clearly and quickly.

my	you	our*	maid*
wash*	washes*	we	oil*
water	of	the	are
her	they	come	she

* Red Word in this book only

This is my house.

Let's look round.
I will tell you
about my house.

The kitchen

Our cook cooks our food in this room.

This is my cat, Patch. Patch has found a mouse!

The scullery

Our maid washes our shirts and dresses in this room.

mangle

She **squeezes** out the water **in the mangle.**

The **sitting room**

We sit and sing songs in this room.

I play with my rocking horse and my scrapbook.

My bedroom

I sleep in this room. Can you see the oil lamp?

The bathroom

We wash in a bowl, with water from a jug.

The lav is out in the garden.

The garden

I play with my spinning top
in the garden with Sid.

This is us sitting on the couch.
We feel proud of our house!

Questions to talk about

Ask children to TTYP for each question using 'Fastest finger' (FF) or 'Have a think' (HaT).

p.10 (FF)   Who is Patch?

p.11 (FF)   Where does the maid do the washing?

p.13 (FF)   What lights up the bedroom?

p.14 (FF)   What does Jim use to have a wash?

p.16 (HaT)   Does Jim like his house?

Questions to read and answer

(Children complete without your help.)

1. The cook cooks food in the **garden** / **kitchen** / **bedroom**.

2. Patch has found a **house** / **couch** / **mouse**.

3. Jim **sings** / **plays** / **sleeps** in the bedroom.

4. The lav is in the **garden** / **bathroom** / **house**.

5. Jim plays with a wooden **horse** / **doll** / **mouse**.